MW00824946

PSYCHEDELIC ORIGAMI

Duy Nguyen & Robert Fathauer

STERLING INNOVATION
An imprint of Sterling Publishing Co., Inc.

New York / London
www.sterlingpublishing.com

2 4 6 8 10 9 7 5 3 1

Published by Sterling Publishing Co., Inc.
387 Park Avenue South, New York, NY 10016
© 2009 by Sterling Publishing Co., Inc.

This book is comprised of materials from the following
Sterling Publishing Co., Inc. titles:

Origami Deluxe © 2007 by Duy Nguyen and Robert Fathauer
Paper Creations: Mythical Creature Origami © 2008 by Duy Nguyen
Super-Easy Origami © 2005 by Duy Nguyen

Original origami projects © Duy Nguyen

Distributed in Canada by Sterling Publishing
c/o Canadian Manda Group, 165 Dufferin Street
Toronto, Ontario, Canada M6K 3H6
Distributed in the United Kingdom by GMC Distribution Services
Castle Place, 166 High Street, Lewes, East Sussex, England BN7 1XU
Distributed in Australia by Capricorn Link (Australia) Pty. Ltd.
P.O. Box 704, Windsor, NSW 2756, Australia

This book is part of Psychedelic Origami Book & Gift Set and
is not to be sold separately.

Sterling ISBN 978-1-4027-6692-3

For information about custom editions, special sales, premium and
corporate purchases, please contact Sterling Special Sales
Department at 800-805-5489 or specialsales@sterlingpublishing.com.

CONTENTS

INTRODUCTION 4
BASIC INSTRUCTIONS 5
SYMBOLS & LINES 6
BASIC FOLDS 7

DOVE 13
FLOWER 17
BUTTERFLY 20
PEACE SIGN 23
GUITAR...34
PINK ELEPHANT 44

ORIGAMI TESSELLATIONS

INTRODUCTION 48
BASIC GRIDS 49
STELLAR HEXAGON 51
TRIPLE-TIERED HEXAGONS 55
TRIANGLE SQUASH 58

INDEX 63

INTRODUCTION

Some years ago, when I first began learning origami, I struggled with even the simplest folds. I would look back at the instructions given at the beginning of the book again and again, reviewing the basic folds. I also looked ahead, at the diagram showing the next step of whatever project I was folding, to see how it should look, to be certain I was following the instructions correctly. Looking ahead at the "next step," the result of a fold, is incidentally a very good way for a beginner to learn origami.

You will easily pick up this and other learning techniques as you follow the step-by-step directions given for this new collection. Some are fairly easy to fold, formed from only a single square of paper. Others may call for a good deal more time and effort, with smaller and tighter folds to add creative detail. But if you persevere, I guarantee the result will most certainly be worth it.

—Duy Nguyen

BASIC INSTRUCTIONS

PAPER

Paper used in traditional origami is thin, keeps a crease well, and folds flat. Packets of specially designed sheets, about 6 and 8 inches square (15 and 21 cm), are available in various colors. You can use plain white, solid-color, or even wrapping paper with a design only on one side and cut to size. Be aware, though, that some papers stretch slightly in length or width, which can cause folding problems, while others tear easily.

Beginners, or those concerned about getting their fingers to work tight folds, might consider using larger paper sizes. Regular paper may be too heavy to allow the many tight folds needed in creating more traditional origami figures, with many folds, but fine for larger versions of these intriguing projects. So sit down, select some paper, and begin to fold and enjoy the wonderful art that is origami.

GLUE

Use an easy-flowing but not loose paper glue. Use it sparingly; don't soak the paper. A flat toothpick makes a good applicator. Be sure to allow the glued form time to dry. Avoid stick glue, which can become overly dry and crease or damage your figure.

TECHINQUE

Fold with care. Position the paper precisely, especially at corners, and line edges up before creasing. Once you are sure of the fold, use a fingernail to make a clean, flat crease.

For more complex folds, create "construction lines." Fold and unfold, using simple mountain and valley folds, to pre-crease. This creates guidelines, and the finished fold is more likely to match the one shown in the book. Folds that look different, because the angles are slightly different, can throw you off. Don't get discouraged with your first efforts. In time, what your mind can create, your fingers can fashion.

SYMBOLS & LINES

FOLD LINES

valley   – – – – – – – – – – – – – – – –

mountain   –··–··–··–··–··–··–··–

Cut line   ┼┼┼┼┼┼┼┼┼┼┼┼┼┼┼┼┼┼┼┼┼┼┼

Turn over or rotate

Fold then unfold   ←————→

Pleat fold
(repeated folding)

Crease line   ————————————————

SQUARING OFF PAPER

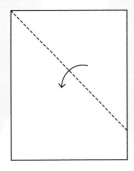

1. Take a rectangular sheet of paper and valley fold it diagonally to opposite edge.

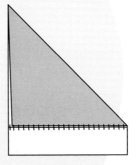

2. Cut off excess on long side as shown.

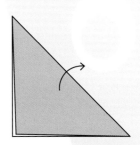

3. Unfold, and sheet is square.

BASIC FOLDS

KITE FOLD

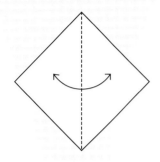

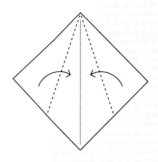

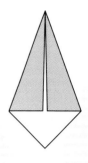

1. Fold and unfold a square diagonally, making a center crease.

2. Fold both sides in to the center crease.

3. This is a kite form.

VALLEY FOLD

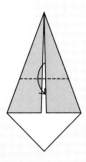

1. Here, using the kite, fold form toward you (forward), making a "valley."

2. This fold forward is a valley fold.

MOUNTAIN FOLD

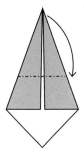

1. Here, using the kite, fold form away from you (backward), making a "mountain."

2. This fold backward is a mountain fold.

INSIDE REVERSE FOLD

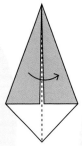  

1. Starting here with a kite, valley fold kite closed.

2. Valley fold as marked to crease, then unfold.

3. Pull tip in direction of arrow.

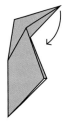 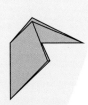

4. Appearance before completion.

5. You've made an inside reverse fold.

OUTSIDE REVERSE FOLD

1. Using closed kite, valley fold, then unfold.

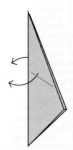

2. Fold inside out, as shown by arrows.

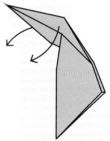

3. Appearance before completion.

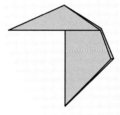

4. You've made an outside reverse fold.

PLEAT FOLD

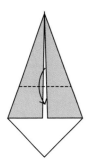

1. Here, using the kite, valley fold.

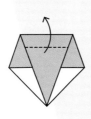

2. Valley fold back again.

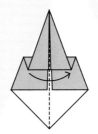

3. This is a pleat. Valley fold in half.

4. This is a pleat fold.

PLEAT FOLD REVERSE

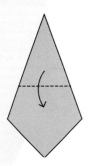

1. Here, using the kite form backward, valley fold.

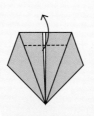

2. Valley fold back again for pleat.

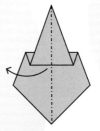

3. Mountain fold form in half.

4. This is a pleat fold reverse.

SQUASH FOLD I

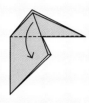

1. Using inside reverse, valley fold one side.

2. This is a squash fold I.

SQUASH FOLD II

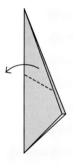

1. Using closed kite form, valley fold.

2. Open in direction of the arrow.

3. Appearance before completion.

4. This is a squash fold II.

INSIDE CRIMP FOLD

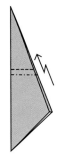

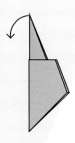

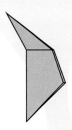

1. Here using closed kite form, pleat fold.

2. Pull tip in direction of the arrow.

3. This is an inside crimp fold.

OUTSIDE CRIMP FOLD

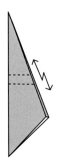

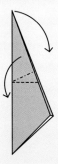

1. Here using closed kite form, pleat fold and unfold.

2. Fold mountain and valley as shown, both sides.

3. This is an outside crimp fold.

DOVE

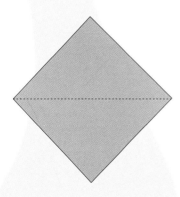

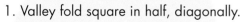

1. Valley fold square in half, diagonally.

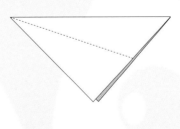

2. Valley folds to half of baseline, front and back.

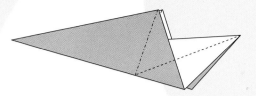

3. Valley folds front and back, and squash fold as you go.

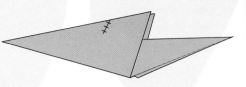

4. Cuts as shown.

5. Now mountain folds.

6. Inside reverse fold.

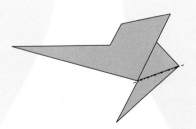

7. Another inside reverse fold.

8. Inside reverse fold again.

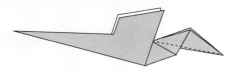

9. Valley folds, front and back.

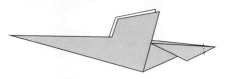

10. Mountain fold, to form "tail" end.

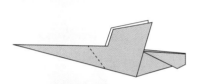

11. Outside reverse fold.

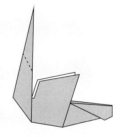

12. Outside reverse fold.

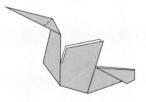

13. Outside reverse fold.

14. Completed fold, see close-ups for head detail.

15. Pull to sides and flatten.

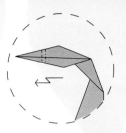

16. Pleat fold.

17. Return to full view.

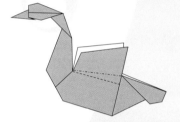

18. Pleat fold "wings" front and back.

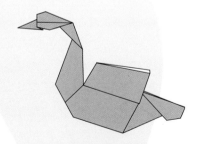

19. Completed Dove.

FLOWER

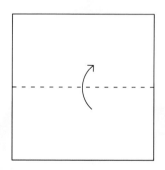

1. Valley fold.

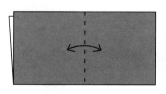

2. Valley fold and unfold.

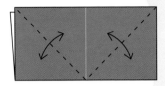

3. Valley fold and unfold again.

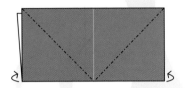

4. Inside reverse folds.

5. Inside reverse folds again.

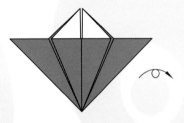

6. Turn over.

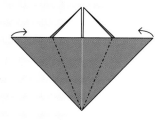

7. Inside reverse folds.

8. Open up the folds slightly.

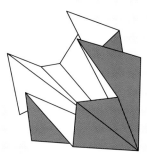

9. Completed Flower.

BUTTERFLY

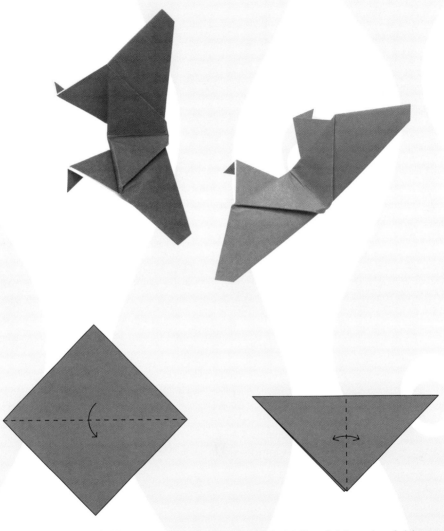

1. Valley fold.

2. Valley fold and unfold.

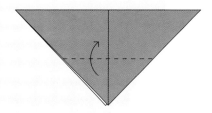

3. Valley fold both layers together.

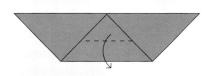

4. Valley fold both layers together.

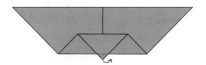

5. Mountain fold.

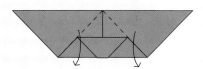

6. Valley folds.

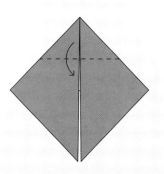

7. Valley fold.

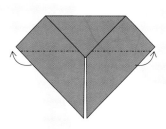

8. Mountain folds.

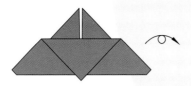 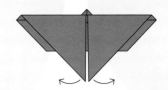

9. Turn over.

10. Pull the sides outward. Squash fold.

11. Valley folds.

12. Valley fold and unfold.

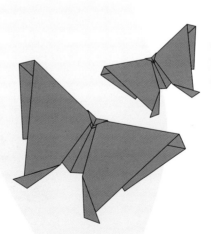

13. Completed Butterfly.

PEACE SIGN

PART 1

1. Mountain fold bottom.

2. Valley fold and unfold.

3. Valley folds.

4. Valley folds.

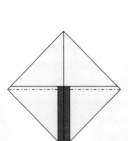

5. Mountain fold.

6. Valley folds and unfolds.

7. Inside reverse folds.

8. Completed part 1. Repeat steps 1 through 7 for a total of two completed pieces.

PART 2

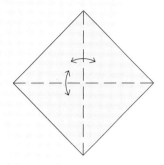

1. Valley folds and unfolds.

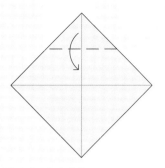

2. Valley fold.

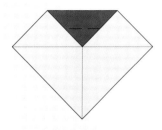

3. Valley fold.

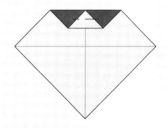

4. Valley fold.

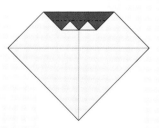

5. Mountain fold.

6. Mountain fold.

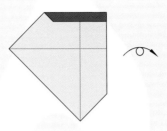

7. Turn over.

8. Valley fold and unfold.

9. Valley fold.

10. Valley fold.

11. Valley fold.

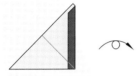

12. Rotate clockwise.

13. Valley folds and unfolds.

14. Inside reverse folds.

15. Completed part 2. Repeat steps 1 through 14 for a total of two completed pieces.

ASSEMBLY 1

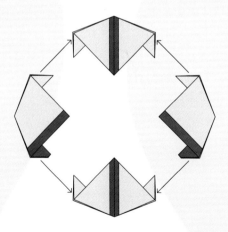

1. Insert all part 1 pieces into part 2 pieces as shown. Apply glue to hold.

2. Completed assembly 1.

PART 3

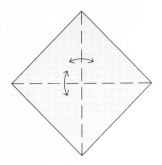

1. Valley folds and unfolds.

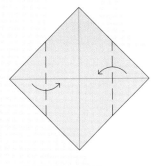

2. Valley folds.

3. Valley folds.

4. Valley folds.

5. Valley folds.

6. Mountain folds.

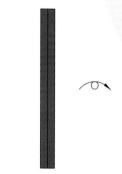

7. Turn over.

8. Unfold.

9. Pleat folds.

10. Mountain fold.

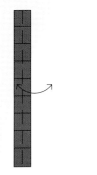

11. Valley fold and unfold.

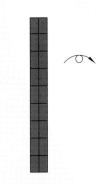

12. Turn over.

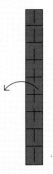

13. Valley fold.

14. Pull and fold at the top.

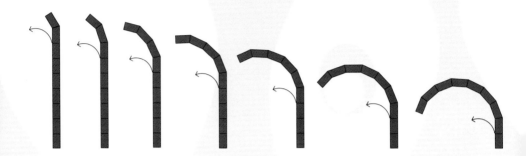

15. Pull and fold seven more times to create a half circle.

16. Completed part 3. Repeat steps 1 through 15 for a total of two completed pieces.

ASSEMBLY 2

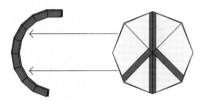 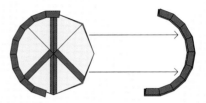

1. Insert assembly 1 into the inside folds of part 3. Apply glue to hold.

2. Completed Peace Sign.

GUITAR

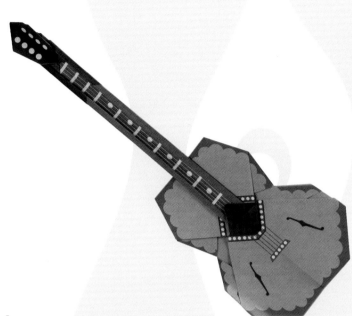

PART 1

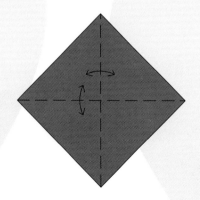

1. Valley folds and unfolds.

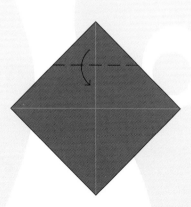

2. Valley fold.

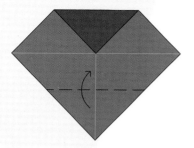

3. Valley fold.

4. Turn over.

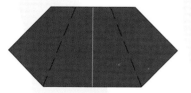

5. Valley folds.

6. Valley folds.

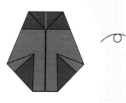

7. Turn over.

8. Cuts and valley folds.

9. Hide corners behind top flap.

10. Mountain folds.

11. Valley fold.

12. Hide valley fold behind top flap.

13. Valley fold.

14. Valley fold.

15. Inside reverse fold.

16. Unfold.

17. Completed part 1.

PART 2

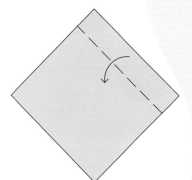

1. Valley fold.

2. Valley fold.

3. Valley fold.

4. Pull paper out and flatten.

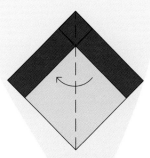

5. Valley fold.

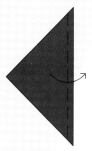

6. Valley fold.

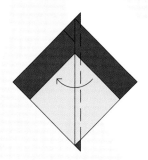

7. Valley fold.

8. Turn over.

9. Valley fold.

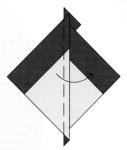

10. Valley fold.

11. Valley fold.

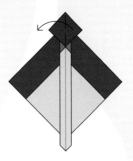

12. Valley fold.

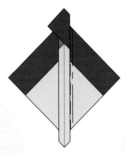

13. Pleat fold.

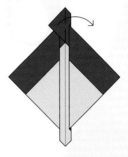

14. Valley fold.

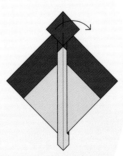

15. Valley fold.

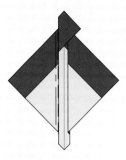

16. Pleat fold.

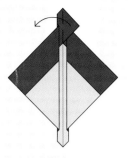

17. Valley fold.

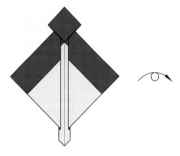

18. Turn over.

19. Cuts and valley fold.

20. Valley fold.

21. Valley folds.

22. Hide behind.

23. Turn over.

24. Crease down the center.

25. Completed part 2.

ASSEMBLY

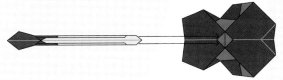

1. Insert part 2 into part 1 as shown and apply glue to hold.

2. Add colors and patterns if desired.

3. Completed Guitar.

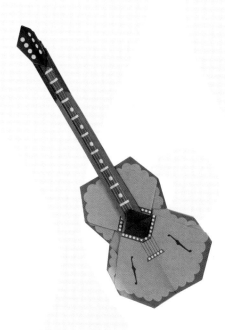

PINK ELEPHANT

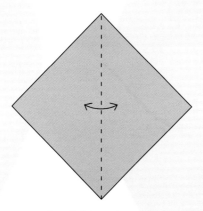

1. Valley fold and unfold.

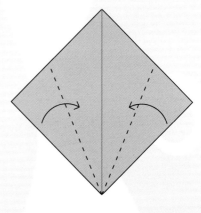

2. Valley folds.

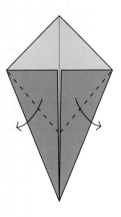

3. Now make these two valley folds.

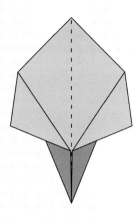

4. Valley fold the form in half.

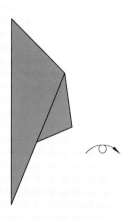

5. Rotate clockwise.

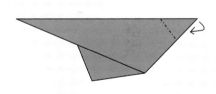

6. Inside reverse fold.

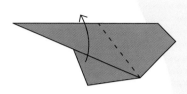

7. Outside reverse fold.

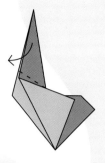

8. Outside reverse fold.

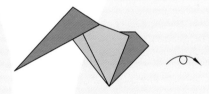

9. Rotate clockwise.

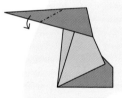

10. Inside reverse fold.

11. Inside reverse fold.   12. Inside reverse fold.   13. Valley folds and unfolds.

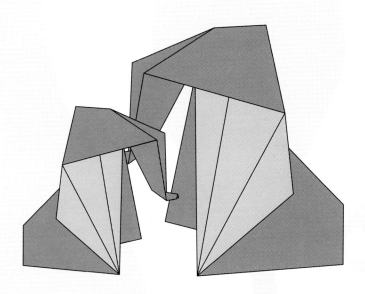

14. Completed Pink Elephant.

ORIGAMI TESSELLATIONS

Origami is usually used to create animals or other figures, as in the earlier projects in this book. Origami can also be used to create boxes and other geometric figures that many people find beautiful by virtue of their symmetry. The remainder of this book will be concerned with origami tessellations, a particular type of geometric figure.

A tessellation is a collection of shapes that fit together without gaps or overlaps to cover the mathematical plane. Another word for tessellation is tiling, and the shapes in a tessellation are the individual tiles, just like with floor tiles. In recent years, creating tessellations by paper folding has been a growing segment of the origami landscape, allowing the creation of beautiful and fascinating geometric objects.

Since an origami piece is folded from a finite piece of paper, origami tessellations are actually small portions of a design that could in principal be extended without end. Three origami projects are described in the following pages.

There are three "regular" tessellations, in which each shape is the same type and size of regular polygon. These are shown in the following illustration; all three will figure in your origami tessellation projects.

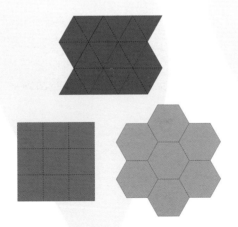

BASIC GRIDS

In each of these projects, the first step is to crease the paper to create the geometric grid on which the particular piece is based. This process is a bit tedious,
but it is necessary and needs to be carried out accurately. To help guide you, the
grids are printed as light gray lines on special sheets in your kit provided for
these projects.

Some of the projects have six-fold symmetry. In these cases, the finished project will
be more symmetric if the starting sheet also has six-fold symmetry. For this reason,
an overall hexagon boundary is indicated for you to cut out prior to folding on
some of the sheets. In addition, mountain and valley folds are also indicated on
the printed sheets, with heavy red and blue lines, respectively.

After folding these projects using the marked sheets, you may want to try
folding them using unmarked sheets. The grids can also be created using an
unmarked square of paper. In the case of a square grid, simply fold the sheet in
half in each direction, use these crease lines to guide folding in quarters, eighths,
etc. as necessary.

To create a grid of equilateral triangles, follow the steps outlined in Illustration 1-2:

1. Book fold the sheet to create creases at the ends of a centerline.

2. Valley fold to crease "a" to obtain crease "b" $\frac{1}{4}$ of the way across the sheet.

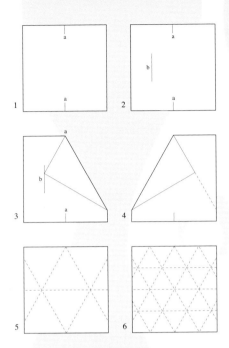

3. Fold a corner to crease "b," using crease "a" as a guide point.

4. Fold the opposing corner, using the crease just created as a guide.

5. Rotate the sheet 180° and repeat steps 3 and 4. Then fold the sheet in half, top to bottom.

6. Fold in quarters top to bottom. Then use the intersections of the crease lines to guide folding of additional diagonal creases. Repeat this step for eighths, sixteenths, etc. as necessary.

STELLAR HEXAGON

This project forms a geometric object that cannot directly be repeated to cover the infinite plane, so strictly speaking it might not be called an origami tessellation. However, it could potentially form a building block in a tessellation. A wide variety of tessellations incorporate hexagons and hexagonal stars. This folding was discovered by Eric Gjerde.

1. Cut out the overall hexagon.

2. With the printed side face up, form valley-fold creases along all of the grid lines.

3. Also perform mountain folds on those grid lines with red lines on them.

4. Begin folding the mountain and valley folds radiating outward from the small central hexagon.

5. Bring the sides in, pushing the top and bottom folds toward the center, so that the central hexagon begins to buckle as shown.

6. Continue folding so that the paper twists, bringing point A to point B. The paper will now lay flat as shown, folded in half.

7. Open up the paper to lay the full hexagon flat, with a ridge standing up in the center. Flatten out the two halves of the ridge.

8. Fold any one of the six regions where red and blue areas meet. First, partially open up the paper, and then refold following the indicated mountain and valley fold lines.

9. Fold the other five analogous regions in a similar fashion.

10. Fold one of the six remaining areas. First open the folds, then refold the region so that all of the valley folds go the correct way. This results in a sort of pyramid as shown in the center illustration. Finally, fold everything down flat by making one side of this region tuck behind the other.

11. Fold the other five remaining areas in the same manner, to achieve the finished project.

TRIPLE-TIERED HEXAGONS

This project forms rings of hexagons arranged around a central hexagon, with each successive ring on a lower tier. It can be made as large as desired. The flip side of the finished project is a regular tessellation of hexagons like that shown in Illustration 1-2 on page 50. This folding was also discovered by Eric Gjerde.

1. Cut out the overall hexagon.

2. With the printed side face up, form valley-fold creases along all of the grid lines.

3. Also perform mountain folds on those grid lines with red lines on them.

4. Begin forming ridges by folding the mountain and valley folds radiating outward from one of the small triangles at a corner of the central hexagon. Fold these three ridges down flat according to the mountain and valley folds indicated.

 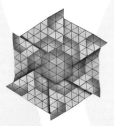

5. Fold the regions at the other five corners of the central hexagon in the same manner.

 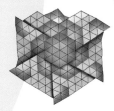

6. Fold any one of the six unfolded regions nearest to the central hexagon. First, partially open up the project in that region, and then fold it back down flat according to the lines indicating mountain and valley folds.

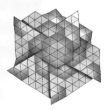

7. Fold the remaining five regions of this sort.

8. Fold one of the six areas at the tips of the six-pointed star. First, partially open up the project as shown in the first illustration, then begin to fold according to the indicated blue and red lines, as shown in the next illustration, till it lays flat.

9. Fold the other five regions of this type to complete the project. If this origami tessellation is extended by using larger paper or a smaller grid, the regular hexagon tessellation in the central portion of the flip side will continue outward.

TRIANGLE SQUASH

This project forms an array of small triangles on the front side. The flip side of the finished project is a regular tessellation of hexagons, but larger ones than those for the preceding project. This tessellation can be made as large as desired. This folding was also discovered by Eric Gjerde.

1. Cut out the overall hexagon.

2. With the printed side face up, form valley-fold creases along all of the grid lines parallel to the edges of the large hexagon.

3. For those creases that have red lines along them, also perform mountain folds.

4. Form mountain folds on the grid lines that are not parallel to the edges of the overall hexagon. These all lie along edges of the small yellow and orange triangles.

5. Form three ridges radiating outward from the small triangle in the center of the paper. This will leave a collapsed triangle sticking up in irregular fashion. The ridges should fold downward along the blue valley lines.

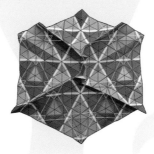

6. Raise up one of the three adjacent triangles by forming two more ridges.

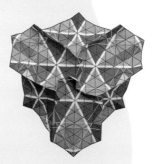

7. Raise up the other two adjacent triangles. The ridges will be a little chaotic between the triangles.

8. Carry out this process for the remaining nine triangles. At this point, the project should look something like the illustration. The flipside should now look very much like the flip side of the finished project (a regular tessellation of hexagons).

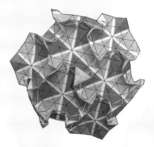

9. Now comes the fun part: squashing the triangles! Be sure all three arms of the center triangle are standing up uniformly, as shown in the illustration in the previous step. Place your fingertip on the center of this triangle and push down firmly. The triangle will suddenly "pop" flat.

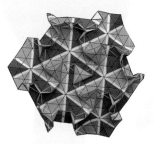

10. Carry out this same flattening process for the three triangles adjacent to the center triangle.

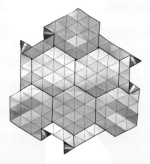

11. Flatten the remaining nine triangles in the same manner, resulting in the finished project. You may want to hold the finished project up to the light, as the light-and-dark pattern resulting from the light passing through single vs. tripled-over portions of the paper will give the piece a different look.

INDEX

B
Basic folds, 7–12
Butterfly, 20–22

D
Dove, 13–16

E
Elephant, Pink, 44–47

F
Flower, 17–19
Folding technique, 5

G
Glue, 5
Guitar, 34–43

I
Inside crimp fold, 12
Inside reverse fold, 8
Instructions, basic 5

K
Kite fold, 7

M
Mountain fold, 8

O
Outside crimp fold, 12
Outside reverse fold, 9

P
Paper, 5
Peace Sign, 23–33
Pink Elephant, 44–47
Pleat fold, 10
Pleat reverse fold, 10

S
Squaring off paper, 7
Squash fold I and II, 11
Stellar Hexagon, 51–54

T
Tessellations, 48–62
    about origami and, 48
    basic grids, 49–50
    defined, 48
Triangle Squash, 58–62
Triple-Headed Hexagon, 55–57

V
Valley fold, 7